I0753800

Series by Stephen Kagarise

Hysterion: Surrealist Love Poems

Zombie Chronicles

The Diary of Madame Rentz

Cyberpunk 1876

Approved Jawbone

AERIAL JAWBONE

AERIAL JAWBONE

Stephen Kagarise

Hysterion Press

ISBN : 979-8-9992019-9-7

"Tu proposes, et elle, elle dispose."

— Lio

CONTENTS

Made Specially for the Purpose

Idle seems a vulgar accusation
to hurl at a man with a business-like air.
Up here in this most inhospitable
region, it ought to be as cold as
Greenland, but it isn't. The weather
has been so balmy and spring-like.
His ultimate object in this grand tour
is to ascertain the vigilance of the
property owner, the new pulsometer
eating raw meat to inspire dreams.

Every Part of It, Nothing Less

Ah, my dear heart, have an eye open
to the future. Let others share thy life's
glad summer glow, when green grass
is stirred by breezes and each leafy tree
shelters many a singing bird. There is
more need of love's supporting arm along
life's slippery pathway, more need for
love to wrap us warm. It will do all you
claim for it, marking with initials only
a lady's name beneath the sapphire sky.

Filled with Enthusiasm and Stings

His eyes lighted up, as if that was
just what he was looking for—a large
bee-hive enveloped in a dense fog.
The more he kicked, the higher he rose
from the ground. He seemed trying
to ascertain whether the 10,000 bees
could see that he didn't like the way
things were going. Numbers were telling
on him. Such humbuggers find the
very poorest sort of comfort in mules.

Employed as a Motive Power

Honest men, with honest facts, don’t
have to resort to sneaking, brutal means
to prove the truth of their case. They
are sharper to see and seize advantages.
They are better men, they work harder.
Consider how they have caused the wilderness
to be populated and blossom as the rose.
Regions that were divided from each other
by long stretches of space, regarded as
the wild home of the savage, now bloom.

This Newfangled Way of Mixing Up

Holders of choice parcels generally
remain firm. No change has been made
in quotations, and the wind was high
but the sun was fair. It would go well with
ice, sugar and brandy, which certainly
fills a real want. He had about fifty years
to serve yet, until the time comes when
they reach the fastnesses of neighboring
mountains. The sky-raking, acrobatic
yelper is getting impatient with waiting.

A Long Rest in Some Pigeonhole

Tempered glass can be obtained in
great pieces, gifted with the power of
resistance. As the demand increases,
that beautiful crystalline substance can be
made to take the place of wood, for
a thousand important and noble purposes.
He has his information from private
sources, which she never had the delight
of listening to before. There is a latent
conviction that he is not dead but sleeping.

Played Too Often at Their Expense

The cold sun showered so many
warm rays of hope. It is, indeed, easier
to acquire than to preserve the very
stones on which we walk. Successive
flashes kept at work in their natural
and legitimate channels, and the chances
of a revival return and remain long
enough. Each party works the harder to
not ask for one dollar. Gentle women
want glossy, luxuriant and wavy tresses.

What Gave Its Fiber to Eloquence

Then was the seed planted, when in
the prime of life she appeared to him frozen
solid from longings. Self-oblivion
came to the rescue, and the magic power
was spiritualized into beauty by her
challenge delivered with a beaming smile.
You would have no chance to slumber.
A trip-hammer pounded out bars of iron
clothed in the brilliant scarlet costume
wont to prey upon characters and events.

As He Had Mastered the Art of War

The firmament begins to tremble,
overshadowed by doubts of his destiny.
A meteor blazes against the sky
behind him, striving in vain to revive
the last dot of rope that holds them.
Again the balloon rises, like a tree walking
through the empyrean. He aspired to
nothing else. Hurrah for our side, twelve
hours sooner than the last snowstorm.
No means of escape, capture inevitable.

With a Store of Golden Moments

How strictly we would look at our
own pockets after hearing the tale, making
very sure that what coin we had as
interlocutor should be well spent one
by one. The tops of telegraph poles
have tasted it, and found it palatable.
When it is fashioned according to
the grade, ball, flake, mixed or tongue,
it is then taken to factory, and there
exchanged for dialogues or charades.

Then a Solemn, but Distinct Voice

Many persons would think it wrong
not to break down self-will by main force.
He is the weaker vessel, if you can
skillfully contrive to delay the dispute.
Making notes of the phenomenon his
excitement was intense, and his rapture
at witnessing the fire extreme. It can
be well imagined how pleased he was.
Instead of saying grace, he spoke to
the dish alleged to contain a gymnotus.

Measuring the Angular Distance

He gives some particulars of his own
observations of Mars, the most delicious,
delectable, entrancing and distracting
of all innocent indulgences. The young
plant sends out branches which strike
into the ground, and from them numerous
stalks grow up. A vista of promise lies
before her, prosecuted with vigor and taste
in design. There is still enough time to
fit out an expedition via the Bering Strait.

Take Off Your Shadows, One at a Time

A descending dove with a fine branch
in his mouth, also a harp, with cupids,
passed from the region of talk to that of
action. It is, of course, needless to say
here, in parenthesis, the two routes among
the three. When a little dark, take off
the lower wing, then the upper, spatter.
She sat at her instrument while controlling
the wires, in all conscience and honesty
rich enough to do so without any trouble.

Enthusiasm Closed with a Medley

A few opening remarks explaining
the object of this music may be made
pleasant also. Words of two or more
syllables exchanged slates for correction.
She varied the exercises by letting
each get the correct position and proper
manner. The cylinders then become
two powerful air pumps, bound over to
await the action of inaccessible peaks.
An ounce of prevention is worth a cure.

Nitrogenized Alimentary Substances

Sparks of fire are discernible as
a general thing. He gave some amusing
instances of the poetry of the future.
Sometimes a few moments devoted to
the all-absorbing question must rank
among the most stupendous monuments
erected by man. This elegant, cheap
article possesses great heating qualities.
Grass and foliage grew in the depth
of winter, interwoven with strawberries.

To the Angry Partner of His Joys

There was a long and embarrassing
pause, chockful of the hand of Providence.
She sighed and coughed, in token that
his ribs could stand no more. Both
sparrows and linnets had multiplied so
rapidly that the joyful nimrod, more
excitable than judicious, succeeded in
bagging a couple, and still continues.
He hugged and she squeezed, and there
is not one who rendered justice more.

Before He Becomes a Morning Star

He was twice condemned to death
and each time he was released soon after.
His life spent in seclusion was clear
and vigorous, a thread she breaks saying
how long it will be before his silvery
locks play a part in this planetary levee.
She will reach her greatest brightness
in the spring, so brilliant as to be visible
at noonday. The amateur astronomer's
telescope will open still wider its rings.

Our Conceptions of the Universe

Numberless cases occur when
the querist would like an answer, but does
not want to put his respondent to
any expense. When does Sunday begin?
When does it end? The question of
antipodes exercised them for a long time.
That the earth was a flat surface on
which the sky rested heaved them into
irretrievable ruin. To some people
such questions might appear trifling.

Forced in Hot-beds or Cold Frames

Women might easily engage in
lettuce-raising. There is little to be
done but transplanting, weeding, watering
and keeping the temperature equable.
If forced too rapidly, the tender leaves
are subject to a sort of blight or burn.
It will delight all who love remembering
when the cyclone struck them, and in
its wise suggestions will be greatly
helpful to reading of the hieroglyphics.

Sufficient to Warrant Its Expense

Gold, silver, and all precious stones
or diamonds are constantly being
counterfeited in the interests of men.
Bought and kept by the ignorant as
genuine, it is the same with this latter-
day humbug, without any conscience
as to the thieving principle. It bears
the impress of romance, to make use
of it for baser purposes. Their romantic
legends intimate a plurality of wives.

A Dose of Carbolic Acid by Mistake

The die is cast. Give us hope for
a peaceful and uninterrupted trip across
the plains. If their honesty is as they
represent, judge that instead of the bulk
of his wardrobe, which he was willing
to dispose of. There is some unaccountable
fascination to some men in the keeping
of a ferocious dog. One very elegant one
settled in his eyes, placed in position
Micawber-like for something to turn up.

—One of the pilots of Victoria, says the Colonist, has invented a flying machine. Lately he took it down to cape Flattery and tested its capabilities. A heavy weight was attached and rose like a bird in the air. Next a pig was tried and he squirmed through the atmosphere like an enchanted horse floating on pinions. An Indian was next fitted with the apparatus and he soared several hundred feet nearer the blue ethereal than he will probably again get, living or dead. All the experiments were satisfactory and the inventor claims that he will be able to direct the movement of the machine in the currents of air as easily as he now pilots a vessel in and out of Victoria harbor.

The Daily Astorian, January 15, 1881

SPECIAL THANKS TO

D. C. Ireland, Publisher of *The Daily Astorian*

and the University of Oregon Libraries

COVER ART

Futuristic Air Travel

by Harry Grant Dart

www.ingramcontent.com/pod-product-compliance
Lightning Source LLC
LaVergne TN
LVHW010946110826
845149LV00013B/2771

* 9 7 9 8 9 9 9 2 0 1 9 9 7 *